MY HEART LONGS FOR

Christmas

Arranged & Orchestrated by

DAVID T. CLYDESDALE

Created by

TONY WOOD, ALLIE LAPOINTE & NICK ROBERTSON

CLYDESDALE
music group

PUBLISHING COMPANY

lillenas.com

Contents

Everything I Love

Words and Music by
ALLIE LAPOINTE,
NICK ROBERTSON
and TONY WOOD
Arr. by David T. Clydesdale

CD: 6

12

we all call Christ-mas!

(*Music begins to "Underscore 1"*)

NARRATOR *(Male): (Begin at measure 2)* It's here again—the time of year that brings a thrill of expectation to the hearts of children and adults alike. A season that is rich and overflowing with memories and anticipation. The slow build up to the holiday is all around us now.

NARRATOR *(Female):* On the radio, TV and in stores—those favorite songs that we've loved for so long because of how they draw our hearts back to the One who is at the center of the celebration.

(*Music begins to "Sing Me the Songs of Christmas"*)

Underscore 1
(Hark! the Herald Angels Sing)

FELIX MENDELSSOHN
Arr. by David T. Clydesdale

Warmly ♩= ca. 116

Do Not
Photocopy

Sing Me the Songs of Christmas

with
Hark! the Herald Angels Sing
Angels We Have Heard on High
O Come, All Ye Faithful

Words and Music by
ALLIE LAPOINTE,
NICK ROBERTSON
and TONY WOOD
Arr. by David T. Clydesdale

21

24

CD: 15

great love___ for me and for you.

*"Angels We Have Heard on High"

An - gels we have heard on high, Sweet - ly sing - ing

o'er the plains And the moun - tains, in re - ply;

*Words: French Carol. Music: French Melody. Arr. © 2014 Celeste & David T Music (ASCAP)/Pilot Point Music/ASCAP.
(All rights admin. by Music Services). All rights reserved.

91
joy - ful and tri - um - phant; O come ye, O
G D/F♯ G C/E G/D G Em D Em Em A7/E D/F♯ A
94
come ye to Beth - le - hem!
D G/B D/F♯ G D/A Bm Asus A Dsus Dsus Dsus/E D/F♯ D/C
97
CD: 19
Come and be - hold Him— born the King of
G/B Am F♯°/A G Am D7 G D G D/F♯ G Em Am/C

Sing me___ the songs of Christ - mas;

tell me___ a - gain the Good News of

God's Gift___ to us, a Sav - ior, and His

(Music begins to "Underscore 2")

*MALE TESTIMONY: *(Begin at measure 2)* In this season, everywhere we turn it seems we find reminders of "Peace on earth, goodwill to men" and yet not everyone is caught up in the celebration.

FEMALE TESTIMONY: I remember the first Christmas after my father passed away. It felt like a party was going on around me everywhere I went—but I just didn't feel like joining in. So much celebration and yet it was passing me by.

MALE TESTIMONY: Last year when December rolled around, the rumors were in full swing around our office of our company being sold. *(Music begins to "My Heart Longs for Christmas")* After all the days and years that I had put in there, was it possible that they would just let me go? Everywhere in town I went there were songs and decorations and happy people and it all seemed to just be mocking me.

Underscore 2

(My Heart Longs for Christmas)

ALLIE LAPOINTE,
NICK ROBERTSON
and TONY WOOD
Arr. by David T. Clydesdale

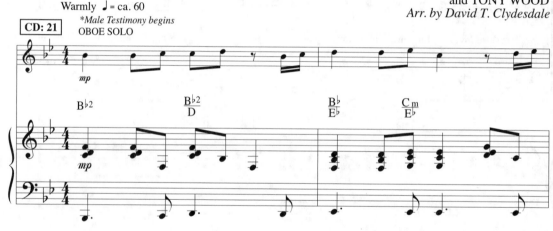

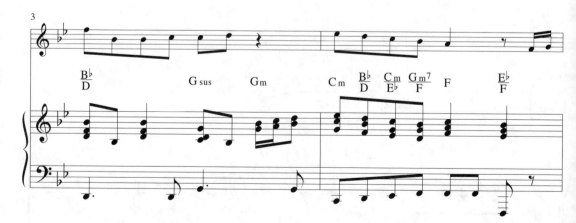

Segue to "My Heart Longs for Christmas"

My Heart Longs for Christmas

Words and Music by
**ALLIE LAPOINTE,
NICK ROBERTSON**
and **TONY WOOD**
Arr. by David T. Clydesdale

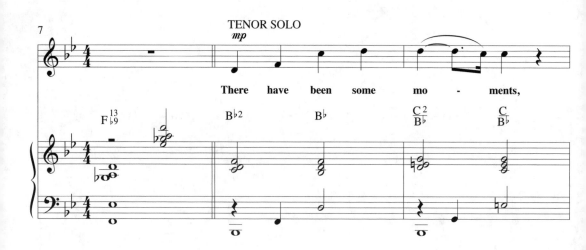

There have been some mo - ments,

CD: 24

for You.

for You.   Ooo   Ooo

B♭2   C/B♭   B♭2

mf   *gently flowing*

For a while now I've been need - ing   some

C2/B♭   B♭2   B♭   C2/B♭   C/B♭

mf gently flowing

40

com - fort and___ some joy,___ the kind I find when

I look to___ Mar - y's in - fant Boy.___ So

I will make some mo - ments of qui - et sol - i -

NARRATOR *(Female):* Mary and Joseph, an ordinary couple living in an ordinary town going about ordinary day to day work. They, like all of us, were filled with longings and expectations for what was ahead. They had a wedding coming up soon. So many preparations and yet in the midst of it all, in an unexpected moment, an angel appeared to Mary and said:

(Music begins to "Call His Name Jesus")

NARRATOR *(Male):* "Greetings, you who are highly favored! The Lord is with you."

NARRATOR *(Female):* Mary was greatly troubled at his words and wondered what kind of greeting this might be. But the angel said to her,

NARRATOR *(Male):* "Do not be afraid, Mary; you have found favor with God.
(*Luke 1:28-30* NIV)

Call His Name Jesus

Words and Music by
ALLIE LAPOINTE, NICK ROBERTSON
and TONY WOOD
Arr. by David T. Clydesdale

Gently ♩ = ca. 72

CD: 27

Lyrics:

Mar - y, do not fear, for your God is near. He has

48

49

*NARRATOR *(Female):* And likewise, the angel appeared also to Joseph in a dream and said,

NARRATOR *(Male):* "Do not be afraid to take Mary home as your wife, because what is conceived in her is from the Holy Spirit. She will give birth to a son, and you are to give him the name Jesus, because he will save his people from their sins." *(Matthew 1:20-21 NIV)*

52

56

(Music begins to "Underscore 3")

*NARRATOR *(Female):* It was a crisis moment for two hearts of faith. Could it really be true? A child soon to be born to a virgin and her godly, faithful husband. How could such a thing happen?

NARRATOR *(Male):* Here they were torn between their dreams, their hopes, their pictures of how they thought life would be *(music begins to "The Road to Impossible")* and this new, different, absurd picture that God seemed to be painting.

Underscore 3
(Come, Thou Long-Expected Jesus)

ROWLAND H. PRICHARD
Arr. by David T. Clydesdale

Segue to "The Road to Impossible"

The Road to Impossible

Words and Music by
ALLIE LAPOINTE, NICK ROBERTSON
and TONY WOOD
Arr. by David T. Clydesdale

Steady ♩ = ca. 64

CD: 38

(Narration continues)

SOLO (Mary)
mp

My

life was full of prom - ise.

Bright

SOLO (Joseph)
mp

My nights were full of dreams.

PLEASE NOTE: The copying of this music is prohibited by law and is not covered by CCLI or OneLicense.net.

6

fu - ture's up a - head___ now it's fad - ing, so it seems.___

C M7   D sus / C   C2 / A   G / B   C2   D

8

CD: 39

Lord, if this is what You've cho - sen,___ I will fol - low;

CHOIR unis.
mp

Lord, if this is what You've cho - sen,___ I will fol - low.

mp

E m   E m / D   D / C   C   C2   C   A m   G / B

64

the road to im - pos - si - ble.

Ooo

The_

Ooo

33

hear Your___ voice___ is a trea - sure worth far more than gold.

hear Your__ voice,___ worth far more than gold.

Em   D/F#   G   C   C/A   D

35

You are God,___ You are faith - ful. Where You lead me, I will go; I will

You are God,___ You are faith - ful. Where You lead me, I will go; I will

A m   G M7/B   G/B   C   C M7 A m7/C C/D D sus D

70

Where You lead me, I will go; I will trust You on this road,

Where You lead me, I will go; I will trust You on this road.

the road to im - pos - si - ble.

Ooo

NARRATOR *(Female):* Mary and Joseph set aside the good things they longed for for their lives in order to open their hands and accept the better things that God had for them. The One who had formed their hearts knew that their deepest desire was truly for more of Him—and that's what He gave them. So . . .

(Music begins to "Underscore 4")

NARRATOR *(Male):* In those days Caesar Augustus issued a decree that a census should be taken of the entire Roman world. And everyone went to their own town to register. Joseph went up from the town of Nazareth in Galilee to Judea, to Bethlehem the town of David. He went there to register with Mary, who was pledged to be married to him and was expecting a child. While they were there, the time came for the baby to be born, and she gave birth to her firstborn, a son. *(Music begins to "This Is the Face of God")* She wrapped him in cloths and placed him in a manger. *(Luke 2:1-7 NIV)*

Underscore 4
(O Come, O Come, Emmanuel)

PLAINSONG;
Adapted by Thomas Helmore
Arr. by David T. Clydesdale

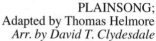

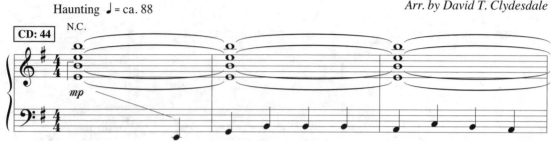

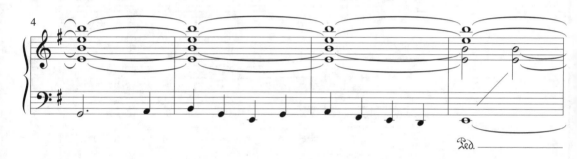

Segue to "This Is the Face of God")

This Is the Face of God

Words and Music by
ALLIE LAPOINTE, NICK ROBERTSON
and TONY WOOD
Arr. by David T. Clydesdale

Lullaby ♩. = ca. 63

CD: 45

Lyrics:
We've known the Name of A-do-nai; we've called Him, "Yah-weh"

78

This is the night;___ we have a face___ to
put with the Name___ a - bove ev - 'ry name.___ Come and be-hold___ Him, this
Child in the hay___ is the One that the an - gels bow down to praise! The

CD: 51

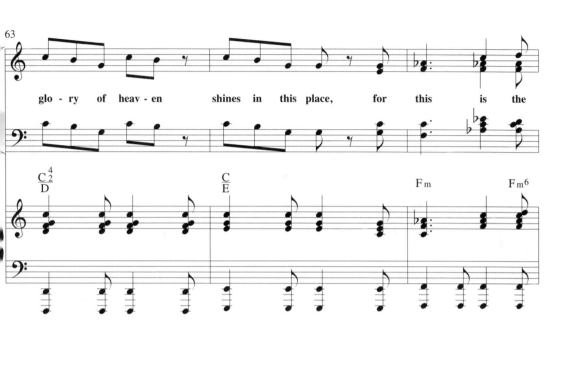

glo - ry of heav - en   shines in this place,   for   this   is   the

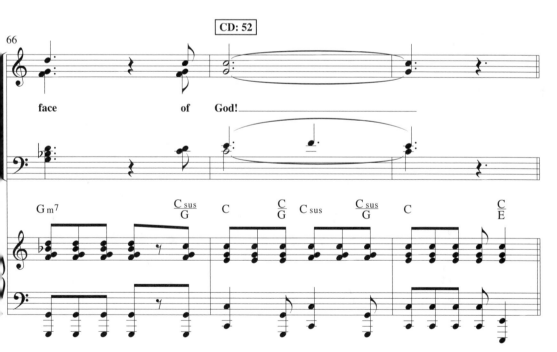

CD: 52

face   of God!

CD: 53

wrapped in flesh.

This is the night;

wrapped in flesh.

G sus   A♭sus   A♭ G♭/A♭ A♭   Fm/D♭ D♭   *Drums play thru*

we have a face___ to put with the Name___ a - bove ev -'ry name.___

A♭ A♭sus   A♭/B♭ B♭m   G♭/A♭ A♭   G♭/A♭ A♭

Come and be-hold___ Him, this Child in the hay___ is the

Fm/D♭ D♭   A♭ A♭sus

84

94

for this is the Face of

God!

NARRATOR *(Female):* Not only were Mary and Joseph given the unthinkable opportunity of looking upon the face of God, but also shepherds and later wise men from the east came to worship and bow down before heaven's King.

NARRATOR *(Male):* They marveled at the divine privilege they had been granted. *(Music begins to "Heaven Has Heard Our Hearts")* Along with all the faithful children of Israel, they had been crying out for a Messiah. And now they knew that God had heard and answered.

Heaven Has Heard Our Hearts

with
Come, Thou Long-Expected Jesus
O Come, O Come, Emmanuel

Words and Music by
ALLIE LAPOINTE,
NICK ROBERTSON
and TONY WOOD
Arr. by David T. Clydesdale

88

*"Come, Thou Long-Expected Jesus"

Come, Thou long - ex - pect - ed Je - sus,

Born to set Thy peo - ple free.

Born to set Thy peo - ple free.

94

70

art; Dear_____ de - sire_____ of ev - 'ry

art;_____

B♭sus B♭ B♭7/A♭ E♭/G   Fm/A♭   E♭/B♭ Cm E♭/G

74

na - tion, Joy of ev - 'ry

Joy of ev - 'ry

B♭sus B♭/A♭ E♭/G   A♭ E♭/B♭ A♭/C

*"O Come, O Come, Emmanuel"

come, O come, Em - man - u - el   And   ran - som cap - tive

LADIES *unis.* *mf*

And   ran - som cap - tive

Is - ra - el,   That mourns in lone - ly ex - ile

Is - ra - el,

100

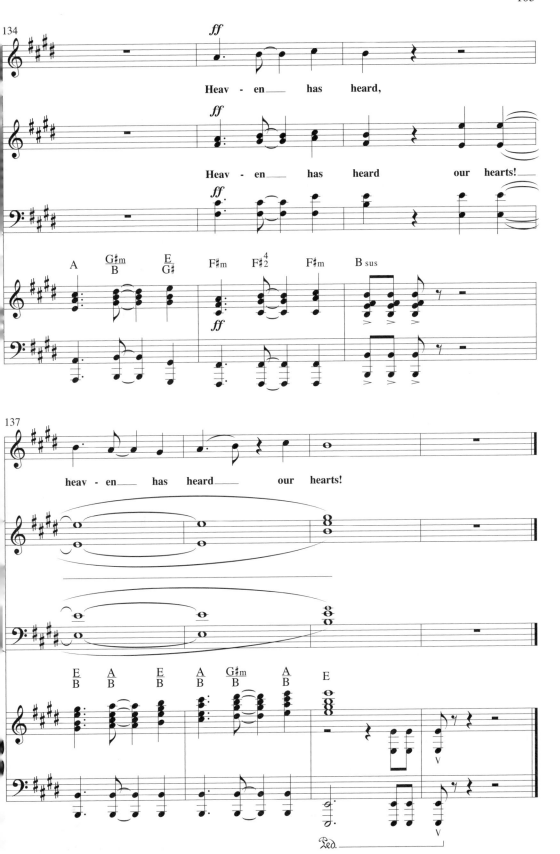

Underscore 5
(Heaven Has Heard Our Hearts *with* Away in a Manger)

ALLIE LAPOINTE,
NICK ROBERTSON
and TONY WOOD
Arr. by David T. Clydesdale

*NARRATOR *(Female): (Begin at measure 17)* So we all come to the manger, and stand alongside Mary, Joseph, the wise men and shepherds. We bring our joys, our hopes, our lives, our failures, our needs and our longings. And we find here, in an unexpected place, that our God has heard us. He knows us and most of all . . . He loves us. *("Underscore 5" ends, spoken dry)* He has met our deepest longings within with the perfect answer— *(music begins to "All You Are")* a Savior who is not only everything we want but everything we need.

**Music by James R. Murray. Arr. © 2014 Celeste & David T Music (ASCAP)/Pilot Point Music/ASCAP (All rights admin. by Music Services).

All You Are

Words and Music by
ALLIE LAPOINTE,
NICK ROBERTSON
and TONY WOOD
Arr. by David T. Clydesdale

Gently, with reverence ♩ = ca. 100
(Narration continues)

hole the shape of heav-en noth-ing here on earth can fill. There's an

ach-ing deep in-side us; we are rest-less un-til: We

re-al-ize the rea-son for the hol-low in our hearts.

116

need is_____ all You_____ are." Ooo_____

(Music begins to "Jesus, Only Jesus")

NARRATOR *(Male):* He is here! He is with us now!

NARRATOR *(Female):* A Savior from our sin. A Deliverer from our bondage.

NARRATOR *(Male):* A Shelter from our shame. Our Hope of heaven.

NARRATOR *(Female):* This is our season to rejoice. Unto us a Savior has been born.

NARRATOR *(Male):* Our God in heaven has met our deepest longings. His answer . . .

BOTH: Jesus, only Jesus!

Jesus, Only Jesus

Words and Music by
KRISTIAN STANFILL, MATT REDMAN,
NATHAN NOCKELS, CHRISTY NOCKELS,
CHRIS TOMLIN and TONY WOOD
Arr. by David T. Clydesdale

keys____ that set us free? He paid it all____ to bring us peace,

Gm   Gm   E♭2(no3)   B♭/D

CD: 82

32

Je - sus, on - ly Je - sus.____

E♭2/C   F(no3)   B♭(no3)   B♭(no3)   B♭/D

35   *mf* CONG. *may join*

Ho - ly King, Al - might - y Lord, saints and an - gels

mf

E♭2   E♭   B♭/D   E♭   E♭6 E♭M7

mf

all a - dore. I join with them and bow be - fore

Je - sus, on - ly Je - sus!

Who can com - mand the high - est

praise? Who has the Name___ a-bove all names? You stand a-lone, I stand a-

mazed, Je - sus, on - ly Je - sus!___

Ho - ly King, Al - might - y Lord,